SPORTS' GREATEST RIVALRIES

GIANTS vs. COWBOYS

Matthew Monteverde

PowerKiDS press

New York

Published in 2014 by The Rosen Publishing Group, Inc.
29 East 21st Street, New York, NY 10010

Copyright © 2014 by The Rosen Publishing Group, Inc.

All rights reserved. No part of this book may be reproduced in any form without permission in writing from the publisher, except by a reviewer.

First Edition

Editor: Dean Galiano
Book Design: Matthew Monteverde

Photo Credits: Cover (front, top) Jeff Zelevansky/Getty Images, (front, bottom) Tom Pennington/Getty Images, (back, top) Carlos M. Saavedra/Sports Illustrated/Getty Images, (back, bottom) New York Daily News/Getty Images, Ronald Martinez/Getty Images, Jamie Squire/Getty Images; p. 1 Ronald Martinez; pp. 2-3 (background image), Ronald Martinez/Getty Images; p. 5 Al Bello/Getty Images; p. 6 (left/right) Focus On Sport/Getty Images; p. 7 Sports Illustrated/Getty Images; p. 9 All Bello/Getty Images, (inset) Jason Wise/Getty Images; p. 11 Sporting News/Getty Images; p. 12 (right) George Rose/Getty Images; (left) George Gojkovich/Getty Images; p. 13 (left) Allen Dean Steele/Getty Images, (right) Mike Powell/Getty Images; p. 15 Rick Stewart/Getty Images; p. 17 Roland Martinez/Getty Images; p. 18 (left) Al Bello/Getty Images, (right) Jim McIsaac/Getty Images; p. 19 Tom Pennington/Getty Images.

Library of Congress Cataloging-in-Publication Data

Monteverde, Matthew.
 Giants vs. Cowboys / by Matthew Monteverde. -- First edition.
    pages cm. -- (Sports' greatest rivalries)
 Includes index.
 ISBN 978-1-4777-2781-2 (library binding) -- ISBN 978-1-4777-2782-9 (pbk.) -- ISBN 978-1-4777-2783-6 (6-pack)
 1. New York Giants (Football team)--History--Juvenile literature. 2. Dallas Cowboys (Football team)--History--Juvenile literature. 3. Sports rivalries--United States--History--Juvenile literature. I. Title.
 GV956.N4M66 2014
 796.332'64--dc23

2013006572

Manufactured in the United States of America

CPSIA Compliance Information: Batch #W13PK5: For Further Information contact Rosen Publishing, New York, New York at 1-800-237-9932

CONTENTS

Bitter Rivals 4
The New York Giants 6
The Dallas Cowboys 8
The Cowboys' Dominance 10
Go Big Blue! 12
How 'Bout Them Cowboys! 14
Famous Stadiums 16
Eli vs. Tony 18
Giants vs. Cowboys Timeline 20
Giants-Cowboys Head-to-Head 22
Glossary 23
Index 24
Websites 24

BITTER RIVALS

The New York Giants' and Dallas Cowboys' football **rivalry** is one of the best in sports. This legendary rivalry began in 1960, when the two teams first played each other. Since then, the Giants and Cowboys have played against each other in more than 100 games.

Games between the Giants and the Cowboys are always intense. In fact, so many of them have become legendary that fans usually have to think hard to pick a favorite. For a Cowboys fan it may have been the 1993 game, in which an injured Emmitt Smith helped the Cowboys beat the Giants for the NFC East title. A Giants fan might mention the classic **quarterback** duel in 2009, when Super Bowl MVP quarterback Eli Manning led the Giants to a two-point victory over the Cowboys.

Giants and Cowboys fans have grown up watching the two teams battle it out. As the years pass, the rivalry grows stronger and fans wait eagerly for the next matchup.

The Giants and Cowboys play each other twice a year during the regular season. The teams line up here at MetLife stadium in the 2012 NFL season opener.

THE NEW YORK GIANTS

The Giants are one of the oldest teams in the NFL. The Giants played their first game in 1925. Many Hall of Famers have put on the Giants uniform. Players such as Y. A. Tittle, Frank Gifford, and Harry Carson have helped the Giants be one of the NFL's most successful teams.

Y. A. Tittle (#14) and Frank Gifford (#16) each had his number retired by the Giants. This great honor means that no Giants player will ever wear their numbers again.

Harry Carson was one of the most feared defensive football players of his time. In 2006, Carson was inducted into the Pro Football Hall of Fame.

In addition to being one of the first NFL teams, the Giants are also among the greatest. The Giants have won four Super Bowls. The team won Super Bowls in 1986, 1990, 2007, and 2011. Before the Super Bowl was created, the Giants won four NFL championships. They won championships in 1927, 1934, 1938, and 1956.

THE DALLAS COWBOYS

The Dallas Cowboys played their first game in 1960. Since then, the team has played in eight Super Bowls. The Cowboys won the Super Bowl in 1971, 1977, 1992, 1993, and 1995. Only the Pittsburgh Steelers have won more Super Bowls than the Cowboys.

Several legendary football players have played for the Cowboys. Roger Staubauch, Tony Dorsett, and Deion Sanders are just a few of the Cowboy greats. Each of these players has been inducted into the Pro Football Hall of Fame.

The Cowboys also had one of the best NFL coaches of all time in Tom Landry. Landry coached the Cowboys to two Super Bowl titles. Landry led a string of dominant Cowboy teams from 1960 until 1988.

Deion Sanders celebrates after scoring a touchdown against the Giants. Sanders was one of a rare, two-sport professional athlete. In the offseason, Sanders played pro baseball.

THE COWBOYS' DOMINANCE

The first game between the Giants and Cowboys was played in 1960. The game ended in a 31–31 tie. The games have not always been this close, though. Over the years each team has enjoyed **dominant** streaks over the other.

In the 1960s, the Cowboys were clearly better than the Giants. When the two teams played in 1966, the Giants were no match for the Cowboys. The Cowboys won, 52–7. It was an embarassing loss for the Giants and the most one-sided game of the rivalry.

The 1970s proved to be another **decade** of Cowboy dominance over the Giants. The Cowboys' record against the Giants was 17 wins and 3 losses during the decade. During this time, the Cowboys were perhaps the Giants' toughest **opponents**. They were also one of the best teams in the NFL. The Cowboys played in an amazing five Super Bowls during the 1970s.

Legendary NFL coach Tom Landry coached the Cowboys from 1960 to 1988. Here, he gives coaching advice to quarterback Roger Staubauch.

GO BIG BLUE!

One of the best games between the Giants and Cowboys was played in 1981. The game was played on a **frigid** December afternoon at Giants Stadium. In an **overtime** thriller, the Giants won, 13–10. It was a huge win for the Giants, and it **secured** their first playoff **berth** in 17 seasons.

Lawrence Taylor (at left) was one of the best defensive football players of all time. Taylor and star quarterback Phil Simms (right) helped the Giants win two Super Bowl championships.

Otis Anderson (left) ran for 102 yards and scored a touchdown in Super Bowl XXV. His strong performance earned him the Super Bowl MVP award. Hall of Fame coach Bill Parcells (right) is carried off the field after coaching the Giants to a win in Super Bowl XXI.

In the 1980s, neither team dominated the rivalry. Each team won nine games during this time. However, the Giants had more playoff success than the Cowboys.

Star players Lawrence Taylor, Phil Simms, and Otis Anderson helped the Giants win the 1986 Super Bowl. They also led the Giants to another Super Bowl win in 1990. The 1990 Super Bowl was the closest game in Super Bowl history. The Giants beat the Buffalo Bills, 20–19 in this classic game.

HOW 'BOUT THEM COWBOYS!

In 1992, the Cowboys fielded one of the best NFL teams of all time. Superstars Troy Aikman, Emmitt Smith, and Michael Irvin led the team to a Super Bowl victory. The next season, the Cowboys had their sights on another NFL title. Standing in their way, however, was a tough Giants team.

The Giants and Cowboys played each other in the final regular season game of the 1993 season. The game was at Giants Stadium. Each team had an impressive 11-4 record. They were tied for first place in the NFC East, and whichever team won the game would make the playoffs.

In a close game, the Cowboys won, 16–13. The Cowboys would go on to win the 1993 Super Bowl. Aikman, Smith, and Irvin led the team to another Super Bowl win in 1995.

Emmitt Smith and Michael Irvin helped the Cowboys establish themselves as an offensive force. The team won three Super Bowl championships in the 1990s.

FAMOUS STADIUMS

In September 2009, the Giants and Cowboys played at Cowboys Stadium. Cowboys Stadium is located in Arlington, Texas. The Giants won the high-scoring game, 33–31. It was the first regular season game ever played at Cowboys Stadium. Over 105,000 people were on hand to see the famous rivalry. The huge crowd set an **attendance** record for a regular season NFL game.

The Giants play their home games at MetLife Stadium. The stadium is located in East Rutherford, New Jersey. When the stadium opened in 2010, it was called New Meadowlands Stadium. That same year, the Cowboys defeated the Giants, 33–20, in the teams' first meeting at the stadium.

In 2011, the home of the Giants was renamed MetLife Stadium. MetLife Stadium will host the Super Bowl in 2014. Maybe your favorite team will play in the big game!

The enormous video board is among the most famous features of Cowboys Stadium. The video board is 160 feet (49 m) wide and 72 feet (22 m) tall!

ELI VS. TONY

Eli Manning, a two-time Super Bowl MVP, is the Giants quarterback. Tony Romo is the star quarterback for the Cowboys. Over the years, they have clashed in many classic quarterback duels. In January 2012, the Giants beat the Cowboys, 31–14. The win gave the Giants the NFC East title. It also knocked the Cowboys out of the playoffs.

Eli Manning and Tony Romo each began their NFL careers in 2004. Since then, they have become top NFL quarterbacks. Manning and Romo have each made the Pro Bowl three times.

Tony Romo looks to fire the ball downfield as he tries to escape from fearsome Giants defender Chris Canty.

The Giants and Cowboys played another instant classic in September 2012. The game was played at MetLife Stadium. Romo led the Cowboys to a 24–17 victory over the Giants. The win showed that the Cowboys are still one of the Giants' toughest foes.

As you can see, the Giants and Cowboys have played many exciting games. To this day, both teams remain bitter rivals. They are sure to continue this great rivalry for many years to come!

GIANTS VS. COWBOYS TIMELINE

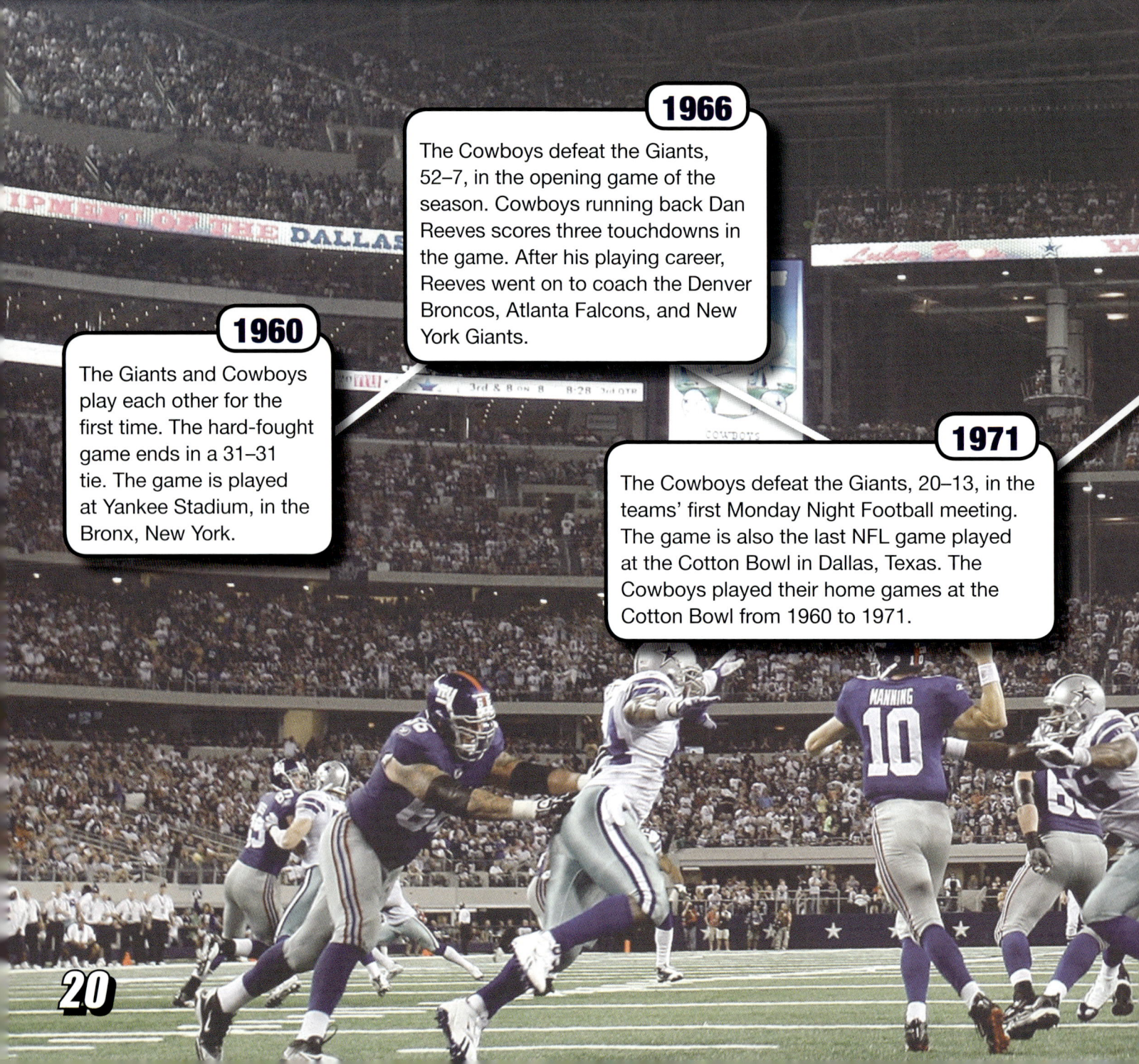

1960
The Giants and Cowboys play each other for the first time. The hard-fought game ends in a 31–31 tie. The game is played at Yankee Stadium, in the Bronx, New York.

1966
The Cowboys defeat the Giants, 52–7, in the opening game of the season. Cowboys running back Dan Reeves scores three touchdowns in the game. After his playing career, Reeves went on to coach the Denver Broncos, Atlanta Falcons, and New York Giants.

1971
The Cowboys defeat the Giants, 20–13, in the teams' first Monday Night Football meeting. The game is also the last NFL game played at the Cotton Bowl in Dallas, Texas. The Cowboys played their home games at the Cotton Bowl from 1960 to 1971.

1993
An injured Emmitt Smith leads the Cowboys to a 16–13 victory over the Giants at Giants Stadium. Smith runs for an incredible 168 yards on the Giants home turf! Former NFL announcer John Madden writes, "It was one of the toughest efforts I've ever seen by any football player in any game."

2007
Tony Romo leads the Cowboys to two victories against the Giants in the regular season. The teams meet in the playoffs, however, and this time the Giants come out on top. The Giants defeat the top seeded Cowboys, 21–17, in the divisional round of the playoffs. In their 100 plus meetings, the 2007 game was the only time the Giants and Cowboys have played each other in the playoffs.

2011
The Giants and Cowboys play their first game of the season against each other on December 11, 2011. With the Giants leading by three points, the Cowboys line up for a field goal to tie the game. With 6 seconds left in the game, kicker Dan Bailey's kicked is blocked by the Giants' Jason Pierre-Paul. The blocked kick ends the Cowboys comeback attempt, and the Giants win the high-scoring game, 37–34.

2012
On New Year's Day 2012, the Giants and Cowboys battle for the NFC East Divisional Championship at MetLife Stadium. The Giants prevail in the high-stakes game and win 31–14. The loss knocks the Cowboys out of the playoff hunt.

GIANTS-COWBOYS HEAD-TO-HEAD

	Giants	Cowboys
Team Location	East Rutherford, NJ	Arlington, Texas
Date Founded	1925	1960
Stadium Capacity	82,566	105,000+**
Number of Championships	8	5
Conference Titles	11	10
Primary Team Colors	Blue and White	Blue and White
Most Valuable Players*	4	1
	Mel Hein: 1938	Emmitt Smith: 1993
	Frank Gifford: 1956	
	Y. A. Tittle: 1963	
	Lawrence Taylor: 1986	

*The MVP award is given to one player in the league each year.

**Includes standing room only.

GLOSSARY

ATTENDANCE (uh-TEN-dints) The number of people at a place or event.

BERTH (BERTH) A qualification for a playoff game or tournament in sports.

DECADE (DEH-Kayd) A span of 10 years.

DOMINANT (DAH-muh-nunt) Being able to beat most others.

FRIGID (FRIH-jud) Very cold.

OPPONENT (uh-POH-nent) People or teams who compete against others or teams in games or contests.

OVERTIME (OH-ver-tyme) Extra time played in order to break a tie in a sporting event.

QUARTERBACK (KWAHR-ter-bak) A player in football who lines up behind the center and directs the offense.

RIVALRY (RY-vul-ree) A competition between teams that play each other a lot and feel strongly about winning.

RUNNING BACK (RUN-ing BAK) The player on the football field whom the quarterback hands the ball off too.

SECURED (sih-KYURD) Got ahold of, or made certain.

INDEX

A
Aikman, Troy, 14
Anderson, Otis, 13
Arlington, Texas, 16, 22

B
Bailey, Dan, 21
Bronx, New York, 20

C
Canty, Chris, 19
Carson, Harry, 6, 7
Cotton Bowl, 20
Cowboys Stadium, 16, 17

D
Dorsett, Tony, 8

E
East Rutherford, New Jersey, 16, 22

G
Giants Stadium, 12, 14, 21
Gifford, Frank, 6, 22

H
Hein, Mel, 22

I
Irvin, Michael, 14, 15

L
Landry, Tom, 8, 11

M
Madden, John, 21
Manning, Eli, 4, 18
MetLife Stadium, 5, 16, 19

N
National Football League (NFL), 5-8, 10, 11, 14, 16
New Meadowlands Stadium, 16
NFC East, 4, 14, 18, 21

P
Pierre-Paul, Jason, 21

Pro Bowl, 18
Pro Football Hall of Fame, 8

R
Reeves, Dan, 20
Romo, Tony, 18, 21

S
Sanders, Deion, 8, 9
Simms, Phil, 12, 13
Smith, Emmitt, 4, 14, 15, 21
Staubach, Roger, 8, 11
Super Bowl, 4, 7, 8, 10, 13–16, 18

T
Taylor, Lawrence, 12, 13, 22
Tittle, Y. A., 6, 22

Y
Yankee Stadium, 20

WEBSITES

Due to the changing nature of Internet links, PowerKids Press has developed an online list of websites related to the subject of this book. This site is updated regularly. Please use this link to access the list: www.powerkidslinks.com/sgr/gntcbwy/